YOU
SAID A
MOUTHFUL!

YOU
SAID A
MOUTHFUL!

Wise and Witty
Quotations About Food

★

Compiled by Ronald D. Fuchs

A THOMAS DUNNE BOOK

ST. MARTIN'S PRESS
NEW YORK

A THOMAS DUNNE BOOK.
An imprint of St. Martin's Press.

Library of Congress Cataloging-in-Publication Data

You said a mouthful : wise and witty quotations about food /
edited by Ronald D. Fuchs.
p.   cm.
"A Thomas Dunne book."
ISBN 0-312-14773-2
1. Food—Quotations, maxims, etc.   I. Fuchs, Ronald D.
PN6084.F6Y68   1996
641—dc20   96-9452
CIP

First Edition: December 1996

10 9 8 7 6 5 4 3 2 1

THANKS TO …

A lot of chefs helped to create this collection of food quotes. Certainly everyone quoted herein is thanked for making this book's menu and our lives all the richer with their words and wit.

But others helped as well, proving that too many cooks don't always spoil the broth. Some offered encouragement and humor—the best sustenance of all. Some offered news clippings and scribbles on paper to stock my food-quote cupboard. Some offered both. These are people whom I enjoy breaking bread with, and all of them—family and friends—are pleasant dining companions. They are the frosting on life's cake and include:

Ruth Cavin, Novia deCarrillo, Gerard deLisser, Mary deLisser, Cindy Etcheverry, Jeri Fierstein, Chris Fuchs, Gary Fuchs, Brian Hoey, Nick Miles, John Murphy, Ellen Piazza, Donald Smith, Steve Sohmer, Harry Stone, Glenn Wolfe, and Eileen Young.

A special thanks to my folks. To my dad, Hans, for being as great a father as he is a pastry chef, and my mom, Margaret, for giving me the right ingredients for life's menu.

And finally to Sheila, the tastiest morsel in my life who day in and day out proves that food is love.

MENU

—

FOREWORD

—●—

Food glorious food, mixed with words of wisdom—
the combination is delicious and goes back as far as
I can remember, always on the tip of my tongue. When
exactly they blended together, like a perfect marriage of
oil and vinegar, is hard to pinpoint.

Perhaps, as my mother tells it, it was when, as a child,
I spent hours sitting on the kitchen floor banging the
pots and pans like some crazed chef hamming it up—
learning to recognize that food and noise were meant for
each other.

Or perhaps the harmony of food and words became
obvious when I first heard about Dr. Seuss and his green
eggs and ham. Certainly my conversations with Mr.
Potato Head underscored my belief in the power of food
as a communications tool. But what probably solidified
my belief in the natural link between food and language
was seeing my sister, Cindy, use her Easy Bake oven.
Indeed, as she baked her miniature sugar cookies I learned
that the power of language parallels the power of food.
Oh, how articulate I became as I buttered her up and
pleaded with pronouns and phrases in the hopes of receiv-
ing one of those cookies. In essence, it was grammar for
goodies.

Today my sister is a professional cake decorator and I

am a man of words—a practitioner of public relations. I have no doubt that we are both better at what we do because we started early. And as I grow older, I also have no doubt that the parallel between food and language remains powerful. As Joyce Carol Oates wrote, "If food is poetry, is not poetry food?" Indeed, food and language go together—like peaches and cream, steak and potatoes, milk and honey.

Food is a powerful language. It can motivate armies to fight and cause small girls to giggle. It can lead to tears as well as cheers. Food amplifies cultures, links memories, and serves as a centerpiece for family gatherings. The truth is, the subject of food reaches beyond bagels in the breakfast nook and picnic baskets brimming with Brie. It reaches the inner sanctum of our courts (the Twinkie Defense) and it permeates politics (How do you spell potato?). Everybody, from Churchill to Mae West, has talked about food or referenced it to make a point.

Which is why I put this book together. Welcome to a bake sale for your brain, a smorgasbord for spicy statements, nutrition for knowledge. This is a table at which both lovers of linguistics and of linguine can partake. So grab a snack and relish words you will be glad to eat.

—RON FUCHS

YOU
SAID A
MOUTHFUL!

BREAKFAST

It takes some skill to spoil a breakfast—even the English can't do it.

—JOHN KENNETH GALBRAITH

Sometimes I've believed as many as six impossible things before breakfast.

—LEWIS CARROLL

Nothing helps scenery like ham and eggs.

—MARK TWAIN

Dunking is proper for doughnuts; it is barbaric for bagels.

—WILLIAM SAFIRE

It is beyond the imagination of the menu-maker that there are people in the world who breakfast on a single egg.

—MELVIN MADDOCKS

My wife and I tried to breakfast together, but we had to stop or our marriage would have been wrecked.

—WINSTON CHURCHILL

The idea that you can merchandise candidates for high office like breakfast cereal—that you can gather votes like box tops—is, I think, the ultimate indignity to the democratic process.

—ADLAI STEVENSON

Marmalade in the morning has the same effect on taste buds that a cold shower has on the body.

—JEANINE LARMOTH

When I was a graduate student at Harvard, I learned about showers and central heating. Ten years later, I learned about breakfast meetings. These are America's three contributions to civilization.

—MERVYN A. KING

If you've broken the eggs, you should make the omelet.

—ANTHONY EDEN

Omelets are not made without breaking eggs.
—ROBESPIERRE

I do not like them,
Sam-I-am.
I do not like
green eggs and ham.
—DR. SEUSS

Hope is a good breakfast, but it is a bad supper.
—FRANCIS BACON

She was so wild that when she made French toast she got her tongue caught in the toaster.
—RODNEY DANGERFIELD

Grits is the first truly American food.
—TURNER CATLEDGE

Sure, sure, I heard of grits. I just actually never seen a grit before.

—JOE PESCI, *MY COUSIN VINNIE*
(SCREENPLAY BY DALE LAUNER)

We load up on oat bran in the morning so we'll live forever. Then we spend the rest of the day living like there's no tomorrow.

—LEE IACOCCA

What you need for breakfast, they say in East Tennessee, is a jug of good corn liquor, a thick beefsteak, and a hound dog. Then you feed the beefsteak to the hound dog.

—CHARLES KURALT

Breakfast cereals that come in the same colors as polyester leisure suits make oversleeping a virtue.

—FRAN LEBOWITZ

Life, within doors, has few pleasanter prospects than a neatly arranged and well-provisioned breakfast table.

—NATHANIEL HAWTHORNE

Only dull people are brilliant at breakfast.

—OSCAR WILDE

Where there's smoke, there's toast.

—ANONYMOUS

Does it make sense to jump out of a warm bed into a cold cereal?

—QUAKER OATS ADVERTISEMENT

Oysters are the usual opening to a winter breakfast . . . Indeed, they are almost indispensable.

—ALMANACH DES GOURMANDES

To eat well in England you should have breakfast three times a day.

—SOMERSET MAUGHAM

All happiness depends on a leisurely breakfast.

—JOHN GUNTHER

LUNCH

There is nothing like a morning funeral for sharpening the appetite for lunch.

—ARTHUR MARSHALL

Lunch is for wimps.

—OLIVER STONE

Lunch kills half of Paris, supper the other half.

—MONTESQUIEU

Ask not what you can do for your country. Ask what's for lunch.

—ORSON WELLES

Hot dogs and cancer . . . So now how do we get rid of all the hooves and snouts?

—JIM MULLEN

Rome is unquestionably the lunch capital of the world.

—FRAN LEBOWITZ

There's no such thing as a free lunch.

—MILTON FRIEDMAN

In a child's lunch box, a mother's thoughts.

—JAPANESE PROVERB

Manhattan is a narrow island off the coast of New Jersey devoted to the pursuit of lunch.

—RAYMOND SOKOLOV

If you knew how meat was made, you'd probably lose your lunch.

—K. D. LANG

The advance for a book would be at least as much as the cost of the lunch at which it was discussed.

—CALVIN TRILLIN

Then, of course, comes that moment during my weekly lunch with the president when he turns to me and utters those historic words. "You gonna eat that?"

—AL GORE

APPETIZERS

What do I eat an hors d'oeuvre for? Because I have a drink, and then I have to have blotting paper in my tummy.

—Constantine Stackelberg

A pâté is nothing more than a French meat loaf that's had a couple of cocktails.

—Carol Cutler

Canapés—a sandwich cut into twenty-four pieces.

—Billy Rose

Pressed caviar . . . has the consistency of chilled tar.

—William E. Geist

Caviar is to dining what a sable coat is to a girl in evening dress.

—Ludwig Bemelmans

I'd like to come back as an oyster. Then I'd only have to be good from September until April.

—Gracie Allen

He was a bold man who first swallowed an oyster.

—King James I of England

Hors d'oeuvres have always had a pathetic interest for me; they remind me of one's childhood, that one goes through wondering what the next course is going to be like—and during the rest of the menu one wishes one had eaten more of the hors d'oeuvres.

—Saki

Swedish meatballs are the mood rings of the nineties.

—JULI HESS

Black olives—a taste older than meat, older than wine. A taste as old as cold water.

—LAWRENCE DURRELL

Olives are Italian passion fruit.

—CATHY CARDNER

SOUP AND SALAD

Soup: what to call a stew or spaghetti sauce that just didn't come together.

—P. J. O'ROURKE

Soup is cuisine's kindest course.

—KITCHEN GRAFFITI

I live on good soup, not on fine words.

—MOLIÈRE

Of soup and love, the first is best.

—SPANISH PROVERB

It breathes reassurance, it offers consolation; after a weary day it promotes sociability . . . There is nothing like a bowl of hot soup, its wisp of aromatic steam teasing the nostrils into quivering anticipation.

—Louis P. DeGouy

His mind was like a soup dish, wide and shallow; it could hold a small amount of nearly anything, but the slightest jarring spilled the soup into somebody's lap.

—Irving Stone

An idealist is one who, on noticing that a rose smells better than a cabbage, concludes that it will also make better soup.

—H. L. Mencken

A spoon does not know the taste of soup, nor a learned fool the taste of wisdom.

—Welsh proverb

Etiquette is the noise you don't make while having soup.

—anonymous

Worries go down better with soup than without.

—Jewish proverb

Food probably has a very great influence on the condition of men. Wine exercises a more visible influence; food does it more slowly but perhaps just as surely. Who knows if a well-prepared soup was not responsible for the pneumatic pump or a poor one for a war?

—G. C. LICHTENBERG

My good health is due to a soup made of white doves. It is simply wonderful as a tonic.

—MADAME CHIANG KAI-SHEK

Beauty does not season soup.

—POLISH PROVERB

No, I don't take soup. You can't build a meal on a lake.

—ELSIE DE WOLFE

Kennedy cooked the soup that Johnson had to eat.

—KONRAD ADENAUER, CHANCELLOR OF GERMANY,
ON THE VIETNAM WAR

To make a good soup, the pot must only simmer or smile.

—FRENCH PROVERB

Only the pure of heart can make a good soup.
—Ludwig van Beethoven

Good character, like good soup, is made at home.
—Anonymous

Salad is not a meal. It is a style.
—Fran Lebowitz

What garlic is to salad, insanity is to art.
—Augustus Saint-Gaudens

I like the idea of society as a salad, in which the fruits and vegetables keep their own flavor.
—Studs Terkel

Our Garrick's a salad; for in him we see Oil, vinegar, sugar, and saltiness agree!
—Oliver Goldsmith

Vulgarity is the garlic in the salad of life.
—Cyril Connolly

We have never been a melting pot. The fact is we are more like a tossed salad. We are green, some of us are oily, and there's a little vinegar injected when you get up to Ottawa.

—ARNOLD EDINBOROUGH ON CANADIANS

Lettuce is like conversation: it must be fresh and crisp, and so sparkling that you scarcely notice the bitter in it.

—CHARLES DUDLEY WARNER

Iceberg lettuce: First grown in a Pennsylvania garden plot a century ago, this oft-maligned lettuce is now a global star.

—MARION CUNNINGHAM

My salad days, when I was green in judgement, cold in blood . . .

—WILLIAM SHAKESPEARE

To make a good salad is to be a brilliant diplomat—the problem is entirely the same in both cases. To know exactly how much oil one must put with one's vinegar.

—OSCAR WILDE

I believe we were the first city in America to omit the sherry with the soup course.

—MRS. GEORGE ROBERTS OF PHILADELPHIA

It takes four men to dress a salad: a wise man for the salt, a madman for the pepper, a miser for the vinegar, and a spendthrift for the oil.

—ANONYMOUS

A woman is like a salad: much depends on the dressing.

—ANONYMOUS

In some circles, I'm as famous for my Caesar salad as I am for my breasts.

—JAMIE LEE CURTIS

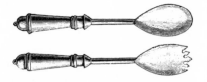

HOME COOKING

When my mother had to get dinner for eight she'd just make enough for sixteen and only serve half.

—GRACIE ALLEN

I never see any home cooking. All I get is fancy stuff.

—PRINCE PHILIP, DUKE OF EDINBURGH

The most indispensable ingredient of all good home cooking: love for those you are cooking for.

—SOPHIA LOREN

After a good dinner, one can forgive anybody, even one's own relations.

—OSCAR WILDE

There has always been a food processor in the kitchen. But once upon a time she was usually called the missus, or Mom.

—SUE BERKMAN

A well-equipped kitchen is an intelligent woman who likes to do dishes.

—ANONYMOUS

Fruitcake is the only food durable enough to become a family heirloom.

—RUSSELL BAKER

He hath eaten me out of house and home.

—WILLIAM SHAKESPEARE

I refuse to believe that trading recipes is silly. Tuna-fish casserole is at least as real as corporate stock.

—BARBARA HARRISON

You just can't beat a woman that looks city and cooks country.

—GRANNY, "THE BEVERLY HILLBILLIES"

I come from a family where gravy is considered a beverage.

—ERMA BOMBECK

Recipes are traditions, not just random wads of ingredients.

—ANONYMOUS

I can't cook. I use a smoke alarm as a timer.

—CAROL SISKIND

Anybody who doesn't think that the best hamburger place in the world is in his hometown is a sissy.

—CALVIN TRILLIN

There is no sight on earth more appealing than the sight of a woman making dinner for someone she loves.

—THOMAS WOLFE

My mother was a good recreational cook, but what she basically believed about cooking was that if you worked hard and prospered, someone else would do it for you.

—NORA EPHRON

The most remarkable thing about my mother is that for thirty years she served the family nothing but leftovers. The original meal has never been found.

—CALVIN TRILLIN

On Thanksgiving Day all over America, families sit down to dinner at the same moment—half-time.

—ANONYMOUS

Sunday Dinner: It's not just a meal—it's a cornerstone of civilization

—R. W. APPLE, JR.

Perhaps the most vital gastronomic role at holiday gatherings is this: Without food, plenty of it and lovingly prepared, we might kill one another.

—BOB SHACOCHIS

A warmed-up dinner was never worth anything.

—NICOLAS BOILEAU

MEAT AND POTATOES

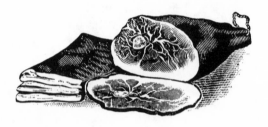

A louse in the cabbage is better than no meat at all.
—PENNSYLVANIA DUTCH PROVERB

Meat twice cooked and a friend twice reconciled are hardly ever good.
—CZECH PROVERB

I believe that eating pork makes people stupid.
—DAVID STEINBERG

A tale without love is like beef without mustard: insipid.
—JACQUES ANATOLE FRANÇOIS THIBAULT

Cyrus helped turn country music into beef jerky: short on funk, low on nutrition, and punishing to the digestion.

—*TIME* MAGAZINE ON BILLY RAY CYRUS

To fulfill a dream, to be allowed to sweat over lonely labor, to be given a chance to create, is the meat and potatoes of life. The money is the gravy.

—BETTE DAVIS

Poor men seek meat for their stomach, rich men stomach for their meat.

—ENGLISH PROVERB

In converting Jews to Christians, you raise the price of pork.

—WILLIAM SHAKESPEARE, *THE MERCHANT OF VENICE*

God sends meat and the devil sends cooks.

—THOMAS DELONEY

Tongue—a variety of meat, rarely served because it clearly crosses the line between a cut of beef and a piece of a dead cow.

—BOB EKSTROM

Southern barbecue is the closest thing we have in the U.S. to Europe's wines and cheeses; drive a hundred miles and the barbecue changes.

—JOHN SHELTON REED

Anyone with a lick of sense knows you can't make good barbecue and comply with the health code.

—ANONYMOUS BARBECUE PIT OWNER

Goat meat will be the fajita of the 1990's.

—SPOKESPERSON FOR TEXAS A&I UNIVERSITY

Spam is a humorous and carvable medium and serves a useful purpose in that form.

—RUBY MONTANA

One man's meat is another man's poison.

—OSWALD DYKES

We had lost our most fertile, food-bearing lands. Without Spam, we wouldn't have been able to feed our army.
—NIKITA KHRUSHCHEV

A few years ago it was considered chic to serve beef Wellington; fortunately, like Napoleon, it met its Waterloo.
—RENÉ VEAUX

Only a rank degenerate would drive 1,500 miles across Texas without eating a chicken fried steak.
—LARRY MCMURTRY

You are better off not knowing how laws and sausages are made.
—ANONYMOUS

Everything has an end, except a sausage, which has two.
—DANISH PROVERB

Carve a ham as if you were shaving the face of a friend.
—HENRI CHARPENTIER

Rock and roll is the hamburger that ate the world.
—PETER YORK

He who cannot eat horsemeat need not do so. Let him eat pork. But he who cannot eat pork, let him eat horsemeat. It's simply a question of taste.

—NIKITA KHRUSHCHEV

I didn't say this meat was tough. I just said I didn't see the horse that usually stands outside.

—W. C. FIELDS

Roast beef, medium, is not only a food—it is a philosophy.

—EDNA FERBER

I am a great eater of beef, and I believe that does harm to my wit.

—WILLIAM SHAKESPEARE, *Twelfth Night*

I never see any difference in boys. I only know two sorts of boys. Mealy boys and beef-faced boys.
—CHARLES DICKENS

Veal is very young beef, and, like a very young girlfriend, it's cute but boring and expensive.
—P. J. O'ROURKE

Not much meat on her, but what's there is choice.
—SPENCER TRACY, ABOUT KATHARINE HEPBURN

Cured? No thanks, pal. Cured of what? What if it has a relapse on my plate?
—TOMMY SLEDGE

Eternity: two people and a ham.
—DOROTHY PARKER

Never go to sleep when your meat is on the fire.
—PUEBLO INDIAN PROVERB

I was always eager to salt a good stew. The trouble was that I was expected to supply the meat and potatoes as well.
—BETTE DAVIS

What I say is, if a man really likes potatoes, he must be a pretty decent sort of fellow.

—A. A. MILNE

Pray for peace and grace and spiritual food, for wisdom and guidance, for all these things are good. But don't forget the potatoes.

—ANONYMOUS

Baked potato—soft, edible container in which sour cream, melted butter, bacon bits, and chives are served.

—HENRY BEARD AND ROY MCKIE

My idea of heaven is a great big baked potato and some-one to share it with.

—OPRAH WINFREY

A man who thinks too much about his ancestors is like a potato—the best part of him is underground.

—HENRY COOPER

What is a croquette but hash that's come to a head?

—IRVIN S. COBB

Potatoes are to food what sensible shoes are to fashion.

—LINDA WELLS

We're serious but not solemn about potatoes here. The potato has lots of eyes, but no mouth. That's where I come in.

—E. THOMAS HUGHES, FOUNDER,
POTATO MUSEUM, WASHINGTON, DC

SEAFOOD

Several years ago, *Life* had a picture story on how to skin an eel . . . I trust everyone cut it out and put it in his files.

—James Beard

Give a man a fish and you feed him for a day; teach a man to fish and you feed him for a lifetime.

—anonymous

Fish, to taste right, must swim three times—in water, in butter, and in wine.

—Polish proverb

One man's fish is another man's Poisson.
—CAROLYN WELLS

Clams—I simply cannot imagine why anyone would eat something slimy served in an ashtray.
—MISS PIGGY

Only a Charlestonian intent on being ostracized, or worse, would make she-crab soup with a he-crab.
—PHILIP HAMBURGER

Ruling a big country is like cooking a small fish.
—LAO-TZU

Haddock: the Cadillac of cod.
—IRENA CHALMERS

I will not eat oysters. I want my food dead—not sick, not wounded—dead.
—WOODY ALLEN

I prefer my oysters fried; that way I know my oysters died.
—ROY G. BLOUNT, JR.

I think the eels prefer to be eaten by someone who loves them.

—SAMUEL APPLEBAUM

Even if I set out to make a film about fillet of sole, it would be about me.

—FEDERICO FELLINI

Oysters are the most tender and delicate of all seafoods. They stay in bed all day and night. They never work or take any exercise, are stupendous drinkers, and wait for their meals to come to them.

—HECTOR BOLITHO

A truly destitute man is not one without riches, but the poor wretch who has never partaken of a lobster.

—ANONYMOUS

Never buy sushi from a vending machine.

—ANONYMOUS

Fish and visitors smell in three days.

—BENJAMIN FRANKLIN

If I go down for anything in history, I would like to be known as the person who convinced the American people that catfish is one of the finest eating fishes in the world.

—WILLARD SCOTT

Some people like to eat octopus. Liberals, mostly.

—RUSSELL BAKER

Fish should smell like the tide. Once they smell like fish, it's too late.

—OSCAR GIZELT

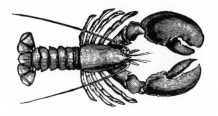

FOWL

When I see free-range chicken on a menu, the first thing that comes to mind is a flock of them bounding across Montana.

—*New York magazine*

Poultry is for the cook what canvas is for the painter.

—Brillat-Savarin

Turkey is basically something college dormitories use to punish students for hanging around on Sunday.

—Calvin Trillin

A two-pound turkey and a fifty-pound cranberry—that's Thanksgiving dinner at Three-Mile Island.

—JOHNNY CARSON

Poultry is like meat, except when you cook it rare. Then it's like bird-flavored Jell-O.

—P. J. O'ROURKE

Don't count your chickens before they are hatched.

—AESOP

What is sauce for the goose may be sauce for the gander, but it is not necessarily sauce for the chicken, the duck, the turkey, or the guinea hen.

—ALICE B. TOKLAS

Jewish mothers dispense chicken soup; southern belles dispense chicken salad.

—MARILYN SCHWARTZ

I wish that there would not be a peasant so poor in all my realm who would not have a chicken in his pot every Sunday.

—HENRY IV

In politics you've got to learn that overnight, chicken shit can turn to chicken salad.

—Lyndon B. Johnson

We didn't starve, but we didn't eat chicken unless we were sick, or the chicken was.

—Bernard Malamud

COOK'S SPECIAL

Simple cooking cannot be trusted to a simple cook.
—Countess Morphe

I like a cook who smiles out loud when he tastes his own work. Let God worry about your modesty; I want to see your enthusiasm.
—Robert Farrar Capon

I was thirty-two when I started cooking; up until then, I just ate.
—Julia Child

The greatest dishes are very simple dishes.
—Escoffier

A good cook is like a sorceress who dispenses happiness.
—ELSA SCHIAPARELLI

Every morning must start from scratch, with nothing on the stoves—that is cuisine.
—FERNAND POINT

The discovery of a new dish does more for the happiness of mankind than the discovery of a new star.
—BRILLAT-SAVARIN

There's only one secret to bachelor cooking—not caring how it tastes.
—P. J. O'ROURKE

I didn't even butter my bread, I consider that cooking.
—KATHERINE CEBRIAN

The most indispensable quality in a cook is punctuality, and no less is required of a guest.
—BRILLAT-SAVARIN

Often, admiring a chef and getting to know him is like loving goose liver and then meeting the goose.
—GEORGE LANG

Miss Child is never bashful with butter.
—PHIL DONAHUE

'Tis an ill cook that cannot lick his own fingers.
—WILLIAM SHAKESPEARE

A gourmet is just a glutton with brains.
—PHILIP HABERMAN, JR.

The rhythm of life changes. Cooking must always change with it.
—CHEF ALAIN DUCASSE

A gourmet who thinks of calories is like a tart who looks at her watch.
—JAMES BEARD

Furniture survives as long as someone has the sense to bring it in out of the rain; cooking dies without the cook.
—DOROTHY KALINS

Cuisine is when things taste like themselves.
—CURNONSKY

A VEGETARIAN PLATTER

I say it's spinach and I say the hell with it.
— *NEW YORKER* CARTOON OF CHILD CONTEMPLATING
AN OFFERING OF BROCCOLI, 1928

I am not a vegetarian because I love animals; I am a vegetarian because I hate plants.

—A. WHITNEY BROWN

Everyone's a pacifist between wars. It's like being a vegetarian between meals.

—COLMAN MCCARTHY

Linked in legend with insanity, leprosy, and even freckles, the eggplant has overcome its undeserved bad press to become one of the world's most popular (and versatile) foodstuffs.

—CHARLES PERRY

I did not become a vegetarian for my health, I did it for the health of the chickens.

—ISAAC BASHEVIS SINGER

Do vegetarians eat animal crackers?

—ANONYMOUS

A man of my spiritual intensity does not eat corpses.

—GEORGE BERNARD SHAW

When we talk about returning to our roots, we don't necessarily mean turnips.

—ANONYMOUS

He who has never envied the vegetable has missed the human drama.

—E. M. CIROAN

Onions can make even heirs and widows weep.

—BENJAMIN FRANKLIN

I would rather sit on a pumpkin and have it all to myself than be crowded on a velvet cushion.

—HENRY DAVID THOREAU

I am a bad, wicked man, but I am practicing moral self-purification. I don't eat meat anymore, I now eat rice cutlets.

—VLADIMIR IIYICH LENIN

The day is coming when a single carrot freshly observed (in a painting) will set off a revolution.

—PAUL CÉZANNE

Sagebrush is a very fair fuel, but as a vegetable it is a distinguishable failure. Nothing can abide the taste of it but the jackass and his illegitimate child the mule.

—MARK TWAIN

Artichoke—the vegetable of which one has more at the finish than at the start of a dinner.

—LORD CHESTERFIELD

Life is too short to stuff a mushroom.

—SHIRLEY CONRAN

If I can't have too many truffles, I'll do without truffles.

—COLETTE

Only in dreams are carrots as big as bears.
—Yiddish proverb

How luscious lies the pea within the pod.
—Emily Dickinson

Cole's Law: thinly sliced cabbage.
—anonymous

The beet is the most intense of vegetables. The radish, admittedly, is more feverish, but the fire of the radish is a cold fire, the fire of discontent, not of passion. Tomatoes are lusty enough, yet there runs through tomatoes an undercurrent of frivolity. Beets are deadly serious.
—Tom Robbins

These things are just plain annoying. After all the trouble you go to, you get about as much actual "food" out of eating an artichoke as you would from licking thirty or forty postage stamps. Have the shrimp cocktail instead.

—Miss Piggy

Where the corn is full of kernels and the colonels full of corn.

—William James Lompton

An onion can make people cry, but there's no vegetable that can make them laugh.

—anonymous

The sliced onions give of their essence after a brew and become the ambrosia for gods and men.

—Jane Bothwell

Kale: All things considered, I feel that this pretty, leafy plant is probably best used as a table decoration—unless, of course, there is no ice cream.

—Irena Chalmers

The artichoke is a trick vegetable.

—Groucho Marx

My garden will never make me famous,
I'm a horticultural ignoramus,
I can't tell a stringbean from a soybean,
Or even a girl bean from a boy bean.

—OGDEN NASH

Abstain from beans.

—PLUTARCH

One man's poison ivy is another man's spinach.

—GEORGE ADE

Vegetables are interesting but lack a sense of purpose
when unaccompanied by a good cut of meat.

—FRAN LEBOWITZ

Current thinking is that the lentil is one of nature's most
perfect foods.

—JON CARROLL

Legumes are truly a culinary treasure.

—JIMMY SCHMIDT

Are you eating a tomato, or is that your nose?
—CHARLIE MCCARTHY (EDGAR BERGEN) TO W. C. FIELDS

Cauliflower is nothing but cabbage with a college education.

—Mark Twain

Zucchini is the workhorse of the kitchen, and a good thing too since there is so much of it.

—Pat Brown

I don't know what it is about men and baked beans, but they seem to go together like an ox and a cart.

—Pam Young and peggy Jones

A cucumber should be well sliced, dressed with pepper and vinegar, and then thrown out, as good for nothing.

—Dr. Samuel Johnson

His memoir is a splendid artichoke of anecdotes, in which not merely the hearts and leaves but the thistle as well are edible.

—JOHN LEONARD ON BRENDAN GILL'S
HERE AT THE NEW YORKER

I don't like spinach, and I'm glad I don't, because if I liked it, I'd eat it, and I just hate it.

—CLARENCE DARROW

Asparagus, when picked, should be no thicker than a darning needle.

—ALICE B. TOKLAS

What was paradise, but a garden full of vegetables and herbs and pleasure? Nothing there but delights.

—WILLIAM LAWSON

Large, naked, raw carrots are acceptable as food only to those who live in hutches eagerly awaiting Easter.

—FRAN LEBOWITZ

On the subject of spinach: Divide into little piles. Rearrange again into new piles. After five or six maneuvers, sit back and say you are full.

—DELIA EPHRON

I like corn.

—WALT DISNEY

I'm the president of the United States—and I'm not going to eat any more broccoli.

—GEORGE BUSH

If fresh broccoli is not cooked properly, then it becomes a big ugly thing, and I don't think any little kiddie or any big president would like it.

—JULIA CHILD

Spinach is the broom of the stomach.

—FRENCH PROVERB

I'm strongs to the finish 'cause I eats me spinach.

—POPEYE

High-tech tomatoes. Mysterious milk. Supersquash. Are we supposed to eat this stuff? Or is it going to eat us?

—ANNITA MANNING

Genetically altered tomatoes . . . The FDA says they're perfectly safe. And people with twelve fingers love 'em.

—JIM MULLEN

There's been an age-old debate on whether a tomato is a vegetable or a fruit. The new genetically engineered tomato is considered a pet.

—GARY APPLE

Most vegetarians I ever see looked enough like their food to be classed as cannibals.

—FINLEY PETER DUNNE

Fine words butter no parsnips.

—WALTER SCOTT

A writer is like a bean plant—he has a little day, and then gets stringy.

—E. B. WHITE

Vegetables are a must on a diet. I suggest carrot cake, zucchini bread, and pumpkin pie.

—*GARFIELD*, JIM DAVIS

Bacon, bologna, and hot dogs are really little piggies who are taken in crowded smelly trucks to their deaths.

—CHRIS P. CARROT, SEVEN-FOOT SPOKES-VEGETABLE FOR PEOPLE FOR THE ETHICAL TREATMENT OF ANIMALS (PETA)

Our schools are rife with gang activity, intimidation, and vandalism, but at least they're safe from the subversive activity of an oversized vegetable.

—RESPONSE TO CHRIS P. CARROT AFTER PETA SPOKES-VEGETABLE WAS DENIED ACCESS TO A CALIFORNIA SCHOOL

Eating an artichoke is like getting to know someone really well.

—WILLI HASTINGS

DIET PLATE

I've been on a constant diet for the last two decades. I've lost a total of 789 pounds. By all accounts, I should be hanging from a charm bracelet.

—ERMA BOMBECK

Never eat more than you can lift.

—MISS PIGGY

To lengthen thy life, lessen thy meals.

—BENJAMIN FRANKLIN

Poor, darling fellow—he died of food. He was killed by the dinner table.

—DIANA VREELAND ON CHRISTIAN DIOR

Many of us don't know what poor losers we are until we are dieting.

—THOMAS LAMANCE

If a fly gets into the throat of one who is fasting, it is not necessary to pull it out.

—AYATOLLAH KHOMEINI

The reason fat people are happy is that the nerves are well protected.

—LUCIANO PAVAROTTI

Everything I like is either illegal, immoral, or fattening.

—ALEXANDER WOOLLCOTT

Fiber: a personal scouring pad for internal use only.

—IRENA CHALMERS

Don't wear a Speedo bathing suit in public if you've ever said, "Jumbo pizza with everything on it."

—CALVERT DEFOREST

A glutton digs his grave with his teeth.

—English proverb

I am allergic to food. Every time I eat, I break out in fat.

—Jennifer Greene Duncan

The best way to lose weight is to close your mouth—something very difficult for a politician. Or watch your food—just watch it, don't eat it.

—Edward I. Koch

I like the philosophy of the sandwich, as it were. It typifies my attitude to life, really. It's all there, it's fun, it looks good, and you don't have to wash up afterwards.

—Molly Parkin

To me, an airplane is a great place to diet.

—Wolfgang Puck

The two biggest sellers in any bookstore are the cookbooks and the diet books. The cookbooks tell you how to prepare food and the diet books tell you how not to eat any of it.

—Andy Rooney

I've been on a diet for two weeks and all I've lost is two weeks.

—TOTIE FIELDS

The most miserable thing is giving up champagne and caviar.

—ROBIN LEACH ON DIETING

The waist is a terrible thing to mind.

—*ZIGGY*, TOM WILSON

I have gained and lost the same ten pounds so many times over and over again, my cellulite must have déjà vu.

—LILY TOMLIN

Dietary fat has become the symbol of indulgence, and rich food has come to suggest weak moral fiber.

—SANDY OLIVER

Diets are for people who are thick and tired of it.

—ANONYMOUS

Never go back for seconds—get it all the first time.

—*GARFIELD*, JIM DAVIS

I never worry about diets. The only carrots that interest me are the number you get in a diamond.

—MAE WEST

HEALTH FOOD

Health food may be good for the conscience, but Oreos taste a hell of a lot better.

—ROBERT REDFORD

Health nuts are going to feel stupid someday, lying in hospitals dying of nothing.

—REDD FOXX

If the doctors of today will not become the nutritionists of tomorrow, the nutritionists of today will become the doctors of tomorrow.

—THOMAS EDISON

I want nothing to do with natural foods. At my age I need all the preservatives I can get.

—GEORGE BURNS

I just hate health food.

—JULIA CHILD

His (Euell Gibbons, the naturalist) idea of a picnic is finding a shady spot and eating it.

—JOHNNY CARSON

Health food makes me sick.

—CALVIN TRILLIN

CHILDREN'S MENU

I like children if they're properly cooked.
—W. C. FIELDS

Peanut butter (is) the pâté of childhood.
—FLORENCE FABRICANT

Vegetables are substances used by children to balance their plate while carrying it to and from the dining table.
—ANONYMOUS

No dessert for you tonight, and don't say I didn't warn you.
—MOMS EVERYWHERE

As a child my family's menu consisted of two choices: take it or leave it.
—BUDDY HACKETT

What is patriotism but the love of the good things we ate in our childhood.
—LIN YUTANG

Childhood smells of perfume and brownies.
—DAVID LEAVITT, REMEMBERING HIS MOTHER

In general, my children refused to eat anything that hadn't danced on TV.
—ERMA BOMBECK

I have been assured by a very knowing American of my acquaintance in London, that a young healthy child, well nursed, is at a year old, a most delicious, nourishing, and wholesome food, whether stewed, roasted, baked, or boiled: and I make no doubt that it will equally serve in a fricassee, or a ragout.
—JONATHAN SWIFT, *A MODEST PROPOSAL*

Peanut butter is mother's milk to me.

—JACK NICHOLSON

A boy is an appetite with a skin pulled over it.

—ANONYMOUS

A growing boy has a wolf in his belly.

—GERMAN PROVERB

Ice cream unleashes the uninhibited eight-year-old's sensual greed that lurks within the best of us.

—GAEL GREENE

Fish is brain food. Maybe if you ate some, you'd understand what I'm talking about.

—MOMS EVERYWHERE

If God lives inside us like Grandma says, I hope He likes peanut butter and jelly.

—BILL KEANE

When we were children, we selected our food on two criteria: what we could trade it for at school and what cool prizes were shown on the back of the box.
—STEPHEN PERRINE

This would be a better world for children if parents had to eat spinach.
—GROUCHO MARX

To the best of my knowledge there has been no child in space. I would like to learn about being weightless, and I'd like to get away from my mother's cooking.
—TWELVE-YEAR-OLD JONATHAN ADASHEK
IN A LETTER TO PRESIDENT REAGAN

I tell children they should throw away the cereal and eat the boxes. At least they'd get some fiber.
—DENTIST RICHARD HOLSTEIN

Yuck, this stuff is full of ingredients.
—LINUS, READING A CAN LABEL, IN CHARLIE BROWN

One food for the rest of my life? That's easy. Pez. Cherry-flavored Pez. No question about it.
—VERN TESSIO FROM STAND BY ME

CONDIMENTS AND SPICES

You can tell how long a couple has been married by whether they are on their first, second, or third bottle of Tabasco.

—BRUCE R. BYE

Condiments are like old friends—highly thought of, but often taken for granted.

—MARILYN KANTOR

Without paprika we have no soul.

—HUNGARIAN CHEF GABOR SZEKELYI

Garlic is the catsup of intellectuals.

—ANONYMOUS

Parsley
Is gharsley.

—Ogden Nash

With olive oil, we are exactly where we were with wine in the 1960s.

—Darrell Corti

If olive oil comes from olives, where does baby oil come from?

—anonymous

As for rosemary, I let it run all over my garden walls, not only because my bees love it, but because it is the herb sacred to remembrance and to friendship, whence a sprig of it hath a dumb language.

—anonymous

Parsley, parsley everywhere—
Let me have my victuals bare.

—Ogden Nash

Enemies to me are the *sauce piquante* to my dish of life.

—Elsa Maxwell

You are what you eat. For example, if you eat garlic, you're apt to be a hermit.

—FRANKLIN JONES

Garlick maketh a man wynke, drynke, and stynke.

—THOMAS NASHE

There is no such thing as a little garlic.

—ALFRED BAER

If I had to choose just one plant for the whole herb garden, I should be content with basil.

—ELIZABETH DAVID

Parsley has always struck me as the culinary equivalent of air: It's everywhere, and thus easy to take for granted.

—REGINA SCHRAMBLING

Parsley, the only condiment you look at rather than eat. Who knows why? But when the parsley and the meat get to be the same color, throw the meat away.

—P. J. O'ROURKE

Wit is the salt of conversation, not the food.

—WILLIAM HAZLITT

I often quote myself; it adds spice to my conversation.
—GEORGE BERNARD SHAW

I believe that if ever I had to practice cannibalism, I might manage if there were enough tarragon around.
—JAMES BEARD

Failure is the condiment that gives success its flavor.
—TRUMAN CAPOTE

Salsa has now passed ketchup as America's favorite condiment. Isn't that amazing? You know it's bad when even our vegetables are starting to lose their jobs to Mexico.
—JAY LENO

Mustard's no good without roast beef.
—CHICO MARX

BREAD AND CHEESE

A toast to bread, for without bread, there could be no toast.

—ANONYMOUS

Bread is the king of the table, and all else is merely the court that surrounds the king. The countries are the soup, the meat, the vegetables, the salad . . . but bread is king.

—LOUIS BROMFIELD

Poetry is an act of peace. Peace goes into the making of a poet as flour goes into the making of bread.

—PABLO NERUDA

If white bread could sing, it would sound like Olivia Newton-John.

—ANONYMOUS

Wes brot ich ess, des *Lied ich sing.* (Whose bread I eat, his song I sing.)

—OLD GERMAN PROVERB

I know on which side my bread is buttered.

—JOHN HEYWOOD

The sky is the daily bread of the eyes.

—RALPH WALDO EMERSON

Man is a creature who lives not upon bread alone, but principally by catchwords.

—ROBERT LOUIS STEVENSON

The bagel, an unsweetened doughnut with rigor mortis.

—BEATRICE AND IRA FREEMAN

You can travel fifty thousand miles in America without once tasting a piece of good bread.

—HENRY MILLER

The Mason-Dixon line is the dividing line between cold bread and hot biscuits.

—BOB TAYLOR

In the Lord's Prayer, the first petition is for daily bread. No one can worship God or love his neighbor on an empty stomach.

—WOODROW WILSON

Better bread with water than cake with trouble.

—RUSSIAN PROVERB

It requires a certain kind of mind to see beauty in a hamburger bun.

—RAY KROC

I am the bread of life: he that cometh to me shall never hunger; and he that believeth on me shall never thirst.

—THE BIBLE, THE GOSPEL ACCORDING TO ST. JOHN 6:35

The creation of bread has to rank right up there as significant to man as the invention of the spoon.

—*HERALD-PALLADIUM*

If bread is the first necessity of life, recreation is a close second.

—EDWARD BELLAMY

Bread deals with things, with giving life, with growth, with the seed, the grain that nurtures. It is not coincidence that we say bread is the staff of life.

—Lionel Poilâne

Manage with bread and butter till God brings the jam.

—Moorish proverb

More eating of corn bread would, I'm sure, make a better foundation for American literature. The white bread we eat is to corn bread what Hollywood will be to real American literature when it comes.

—Sherwood Anderson

Blues is to jazz what yeast is to bread—without it, it's flat.

—Carmen McRae

I bake every night before I go to bed. It's part of my evening prayers. When the bread comes out of the oven, I am at peace.

—JESUIT BROTHER RICK CURRY

You've buttered your bread, now sleep in it.

—GRACIE ALLEN

What was sliced bread the greatest thing since?

—ANONYMOUS

Man lives for science as well as bread.

—WILLIAM JAMES

The first time I ate organic whole-grain bread I swear it tasted like roofing material.

—ROBIN WILLIAMS

Bread is the warmest, kindest of words. Write it always with a capital letter, like your own name.

—SIGN IN RUSSIAN RESTAURANT

A crust eaten in peace is better than a banquet partaken in anxiety.

—AESOP

The bread earned by the sweat of the brow is thrice-blessed bread, and it is far sweeter than the tasteless loaf of idleness.

—ANONYMOUS

Deliberation. The act of examining one's bread to determine which side it is buttered on.

—AMBROSE BIERCE

Compromise used to mean that half a loaf was better than no bread. Among modern statesmen it really seems to mean that half a loaf is better than a whole loaf.

—G. K. CHESTERTON

There is no such thing as bad bread when you have a good appetite.

—GABRIEL GARCIA MÁRQUEZ

I got brown sandwiches and green sandwiches. It's either very new cheese or very old meat.

—NEIL SIMON, *THE ODD COUPLE*

Promoters are just guys with two pieces of bread looking for a piece of cheese.

—EVEL KNIEVEL

A dessert without cheese is like a beautiful woman with only one eye.

—BRILLAT-SAVARIN

How can you govern a country that has 246 varieties of cheese?

—CHARLES DE GAULLE

Goat cheese . . . produced a bizarre eating era when sensible people insisted that this miserable cheese produced by these miserable creatures reared on miserable hardscrabble earth was actually superior to the magnificent creamy cheeses of the noblest dairy animals bred in the richest green valleys of the earth.

—RUSSELL BAKER

Cheese—the adult form of milk.

—RICHARD CONDON

Why is it that Swiss cheese has the holes when it's Gorgonzola that needs the ventilation?

—DAVID FROST

Poets have been mysteriously silent on the subject of cheeses.

—G. K. CHESTERTON

Most cheeses need work. I don't want to be in the same country as goat cheese. It always tastes the way a yak looks in one of those *National Geographic* specials.

—ERMA BOMBECK

You two can be what you like, but since
I am the big fromage in this family, I prefer
to think of myself as the Gorgon Zola.

—OGDEN NASH

There's always free cheese in a mousetrap.

—ANONYMOUS

I don't want the cheese, I just want to get out of the trap.

—SPANISH PROVERB

The moon is made of green cheese.

—JOHN HEYWOOD

Cheese—milk's leap toward immortality.

—CLIFTON FADIMAN

Many's the long night I've dreamed of cheese—toasted mostly.

—ROBERT LOUIS STEVENSON

You put your left index finger on your eye and your right index finger on the cheese . . . If they sort of feel the same, the cheese is ready.

—M. TATTINGER

Velveeta: It's the perfect emergency food. It has the shelf life of stick-on floor tiles.

—RICHARD ATCHESON

Brie with the rind sliced off is among the most essential tokens of yuppiedom.

—STRATFORD SHERMAN

Age is something that doesn't matter, unless you are a cheese.

—Billie Burke

The guy who invented head cheese must have been really hungry.

—Jerry Seinfeld

SWEETS AND STUFF

The only reason for being a bee that I know of is making honey . . . and the only reason for making honey is so I can eat it.

—WINNIE THE POOH

Sweets to the sweet.

—WILLIAM SHAKESPEARE

The cinema is not a slice of life, but a piece of cake.

—ALFRED HITCHCOCK

The most dangerous food is wedding cake.

—AMERICAN PROVERB

America is an enormous frosted cupcake in the middle of millions of starving people.

—GLORIA STEINEM

Older women are like aging strudels—the crust may not be so lovely, but the filling has come at last unto its own.

—ROBERT FARRAR CAPON

Promises and pie-crusts are made to be broken.

—JONATHAN SWIFT

Brilliantly lit from stem to stern, she looked like a sagging birthday cake.

—WALTER LORD, ON THE SINKING *TITANIC*

Qu'ils mangent de la brioche.
Let them eat cake.

—MARIE ANTOINETTE

Once you give up integrity, the rest is a piece of cake.

—J. R. EWING, "DALLAS"

It's food too fine for angels; yet come, take
And eat thy fill! It's Heaven's sugar cake.

—EDWARD TAYLOR

Violence is as American as cherry pie.

—H. Rap Brown

We dare not trust our wit for making our house pleasant to our friend, so we buy ice cream.

—Ralph Waldo Emerson

All this class of pleasures inspires me with the same nausea as I feel at the sight of rich plum-cake or sweetmeats: I prefer the driest bread of common life.

—Sydney Smith

I doubt whether the world holds for anyone a more soul-stirring surprise than the first adventure with ice cream.

—Heywood Brown

The last time I was surprised was when I found out that ice cream cones were hollow.

—Pete Maravich

My theory is that if you can buy an ice cream cone and make it hit your mouth, you can play.

—Tennis instructor Vic Braden

A glutton for cake often loses the bread.
—JEWISH PROVERB

Asking a serious baker to help evaluate cake mixes might seem like recruiting an Indianapolis 500 driver to rate mopeds.
—BRYAN MILLER

You look as pretty as a bag of striped candy.
—JETHRO, "THE BEVERLY HILLBILLIES"

That girl (Elly) is so sweet that when she squeezes lemons, you don't need sugar.
—GRANNY, "THE BEVERLY HILLBILLIES"

I adore seafood, especially saltwater taffy.
—MILTON BERLE

As you ramble thorough life, brother, whatever be your goal, keep your eye upon the doughnut, and not upon the hole.
—RESTAURANT SIGN

People who are unwilling to try new words are the type who refrain from dunking doughnuts.
—WILLIAM SAFIRE

Anyhow, the hole in the doughnut is at least digestible.
—H. L. MENCKEN

Baker's Dozen: Twelve of today's doughnuts and one of yesterday's.
—B. C., JOHNNY HART

There is something in the red of a raspberry pie that looks as good to a man as the red in a sheep looks to a wolf.
—EDGAR WATSON HOWE

My advice to you is not to inquire why or whither, but just enjoy your ice cream while it's on your plate.
—THORNTON WILDER

The best of all physicians is apple pie and cheese.
—EUGENE FIELD

About as much backbone as a chocolate eclair.
—PRESIDENT THEODORE ROOSEVELT
ON PRESIDENT WILLIAM McKINLEY

Why is birthday cake the only food you can blow out and spit on and everybody wants to get a piece?
—BOBBY KELLER

Research tells us fourteen out of any ten individuals likes chocolate.

—SANDRA BOYNTON

Licorice is the liver of candy.

—MICHAEL O'DONOGHUE

The Moon Pie is a bedrock of the country stores and rural tradition. It is more than a snack. It is a cultural artifact.

—WILLIAM FERRIS

If you wish to make an apple pie truly from scratch, you must first invent the universe.

—CARL E. SAGAN

The only true rival the Oreo has ever had in the hearts of Americans is the chocolate chip cookie.

—IRENA CHALMERS

The only emperor is the emperor of ice cream.

—WALLACE STEVENS

My face looks like a wedding cake left out in the rain.

—W. H. AUDEN

You can tell a lot about a fellow's character by his way of eating jelly beans.

—RONALD REAGAN

What calls back the past like the rich pumpkin pie?
—JOHN GREENLEAF WHITTIER

Chocolate: It flatters you for a while, it warms you for an instant; then all of a sudden, it kindles a mortal fever in you.

—MARIE, MARQUISE DE SÉVIGNÉ

Ignore previous cookie.

—FORTUNE COOKIE MESSAGE

Venice is like eating an entire box of chocolate liqueurs in one go.

—TRUMAN CAPOTE

Life is like a box of chocolates: you never know what you're going to get.

—TOM HANKS, *FORREST GUMP*

Had I but one penny in the world, thou shouldst have it for gingerbread.

—WILLIAM SHAKESPEARE

FRUIT BOWL

According to statistics, a man eats a prune every twenty seconds. I don't know who this fella is, but I know where to find him.

—ANONYMOUS

Politics is applesauce.

—WILL ROGERS

California is a great place to live if you're an orange.

—FRED ALLEN

Doubtless God could have made a better berry, but doubtless God never did.

—WILLIAM BUTLER (about the strawberry)

Grapefruit—it's like taking a violent shower inside your body.

—HUNTER S. THOMPSON

A grapefruit is a lemon that had a chance and took advantage of it.

—ANONYMOUS

There is a lot more juice in a grapefruit than meets the eye.

—ANONYMOUS

Beulah, peel me a grape.

—MAE WEST, *I'M NO ANGEL*

So far I've kept my diet secret, but now I might as well tell everyone what it is. Lots of grapefruit throughout the day and plenty of virile young men at night.

—ANGIE DICKINSON

Success to me is like having ten honeydew melons and eating only the top half of each one.

—BARBRA STREISAND

Shape is a good part of the fig's delight.

—JANE GRIGSON

Horses are like strawberries; you must enjoy them while you can, because they don't last long.

—CHARLIE WHITTINGHAM

There are only ten minutes in the life of a pear when is perfect to eat.

—RALPH WALDO EMER

Melons are the sweet aristocrats of the very large gourd family.

—IRENA CHALMERS

When you get to my age, you don't even buy green bananas anymore.

—ARNOLD PALMER

All millionaires love a baked apple.

—RONALD FIRBANK

Millions saw the apple fall, but Newton was the one who asked why.

—BERNARD BARUCH

Your old virginity is like one of our French withered pears; it looks ill, it eats dryly.

—WILLIAM SHAKESPEARE

I'm like certain kinds of fruit: bitter outside and sweet inside.

—SHARON STONE

Ignorance is like a delicate exotic fruit; touch it and the bloom is gone.

—OSCAR WILDE

Since Eve ate apples, much depends on dinner.

—LORD BYRON

Art is a fruit that grows in man, like a fruit on a plant, or a child in its mother's womb.

—JEAN ARP

You can't plant a seed and pick the fruit the next morning.

—ANONYMOUS

While forbidden fruit is said to taste sweeter, it usually spoils faster.

—ABIGAIL VAN BUREN

A banana peel can substitute as a polishing rag for leather shoes.

—IRENA CHALMERS

The white man, when well roasted, tastes like a ripe banana.

—TAHITIAN POLYNESIAN CHIEF

Forbidden fruits taste better than those that are allowed.

—ANONYMOUS

God doesn't make orange juice; God makes oranges.

—JESSE JACKSON

When one has tasted watermelons, one knows what angels eat. It was not a southern watermelon that Eve took; we know it because she repented.

—MARK TWAIN

BEVERAGES

Only Irish coffee provides in a single glass all four essential food groups: alcohol, caffeine, sugar, and fat.

—ALEX LEVINE

My rule of life prescribed as an absolutely sacred rite smoking cigars and also the drinking of alcohol before, after, and if need be during all meals and in the interval between them.

—WINSTON CHURCHILL

Bread is the staff of life, but beer is life itself.

—BRITISH PROVERB

Thirst cannot be quenched by proxy.

—CENTRAL AFRICAN PROVERB

Religious change; beer and wine remain.

—HERVEY ALLEN

Coffee has two virtues: It is wet and warm.

—OLD DUTCH PROVERB

Coke does best in Democratic administrations, while PepsiCo comes to the fore under the Republicans.

—ANONYMOUS

My only regret in life is that I did not drink more champagne.

—JOHN MAYNARD KEYNES, ON HIS DEATH BED

Champagne, if you are seeking the truth, is better than a lie detector. It encourages a man to be expansive, even reckless, while lie detectors are only a challenge to tell lies successfully.

—GRAHAM GREENE

No government could survive without champagne . . . In the throat of our diplomatic people it is like oil in the wheels of an engine.

—JOSEPH DARGENT, FRENCH VINTNER

My illness is due to my doctor's insistence that I drink milk, a whitish fluid they force down helpless babies.

—W. C. FIELDS

There is no finer investment for any community than putting milk into babies.

—WINSTON CHURCHILL

It's all right to drink like a fish—if you drink what a fish drinks.

—MARY PETTIBONE POOLE

One reason I don't drink is that I want to know when I'm having a good time.

—MAE WEST

Strategy is buying a bottle of fine wine when you take a lady out for dinner. Tactics is getting her to drink it.

—FRANK MUIR

I'm a fellow who works in the vineyard of compromise.
—CONGRESSMAN DAN ROSTENKOWSKI

Dr Pepper—Dallas's answer to Beaujolais.
—CALVIN TRILLIN

When you stop drinking, you have to deal with this marvelous personality that started you drinking in the first place.
—JIMMY BRESLIN

The best audience is intelligent, well educated, and a little drunk.
—ALBEN W. BARKLEY

In water one sees one's own face, but in wine one beholds the heart of another.
—FRENCH PROVERB

Some weasel took the cork out of my lunch.
—W. C. FIELDS

One martini is all right. Two are too many and three are not enough.
—JAMES THURBER

It doesn't matter how much milk you spill so long as you don't lose the cow.

—ANONYMOUS

I drink to make other people more interesting.

—GEORGE JEAN NATHAN

Once, during Prohibition, I was forced to live for days on nothing but food and water.

—W. C. FIELDS

This is an excellent martini—sort of tastes like it isn't there at all. Just a cold cloud.

—HERMAN WOUK

I don't believe you have to be a cow to know what milk is.

—ANN LANDERS

The cow is of the bovine ilk;
One end is moo, the other Milk.

—OGDEN NASH

Meeting Roosevelt is like uncorking your first bottle of champagne.

—WINSTON CHURCHILL

At my lemonade stand I used to give the first glass away free and charge five dollars for the second glass. The refill contained the antidote.

—EMO PHILLIPS

The gentlemen did like a drop too much . . . more port than was exactly portable.

—THOMAS HOOD

Gin was mother's milk to her.

—GEORGE BERNARD SHAW

A meal without wine is like a day without sunshine.

—BRILLAT-SAVARIN

A woman is like a tea bag; you never know how strong she is until she gets in hot water.

—NANCY REAGAN (ALSO ATTRIBUTED TO CARL SANDBURG)

Tea to the English is really a picnic indoors.

—ALICE WALKER

There are few hours in life more agreeable than the hour dedicated to the ceremony known as afternoon tea.

—HENRY JAMES

Vodka is the aunt of wine.

—RUSSIAN PROVERB

Those who drink the water must remember those who dug the well.

—CHINESE PROVERB

I never drink anything stronger than gin before breakfast.

—W. C. FIELDS

The House of Lords is like a glass of champagne that has stood for five days.

—CLEMENT ATTLEE

I must get out of these wet clothes and into a dry martini.

—ROBERT BENCHLEY

Coffee should be black as hell, strong as death, and sweet as love.

—TURKISH PROVERB

Or, as the Hungarians put it:

Coffee should be black like the devil, hot like hell, and sweet like a kiss.

—HUNGARIAN PROVERB

Coffee in England is just toasted milk.

—CHRISTOPHER FRY

Tranquillity is the old man's milk.

—THOMAS JEFFERSON

May all your pain be champagne.

—BRIAN HOEY

What Freud was to psychoanalysis, I was to wine.

—WINE MERCHANT SAM AARON

Excellent wine generates enthusiasm. And whatever you do with enthusiasm is generally successful.
—PHILLIPE DE ROTHSCHILD

What is the definition of a good wine? It should start and end with a smile.
—WILLIAM SOKOLIN, vintner

Memphis martini: gin with a wad of cotton in it.
—FRED ALLEN

Opie, you haven't finished your milk. We can't put it back in the cow, you know.
—AUNT BEE TAYLOR, "THE ANDY GRIFFITH SHOW"

Good communication is as stimulating as black coffee, and just as hard to sleep after.
—ANNE MORROW LINDBERGH

SNACKS

Theater popcorn ought to be the Snow White of snack foods, but it's been turned into Godzilla by being popped in highly saturated coconut oil.

—MICHAEL JACOBS

I hate television. I hate it is as much as peanuts. But I can't stop eating peanuts.

—ORSON WELLES

Don't eat too many almonds; they add weight to the breasts.

—COLETTE

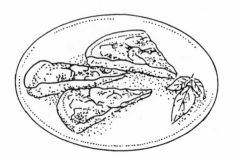

A Chee-to by another name is still a Chee-to.

—JANET SIROTO

For those of you who like to scarf your popcorn in the sack, the good news is that Newman's Own contains an aphrodisiac.

—PAUL NEWMAN

Pizza Hut has a new pizza called the Big Foot . . . and you thought the anchovy pizza smelled bad.

—JAY LENO

There's a pizza place near where I live that sells only slices. In the back you can see a guy tossing a triangle in the air.

—STEVEN WRIGHT

We think fast food is equivalent to pornography, nutritionally speaking.

—STEVE ELBERT

Wish I had time for just one more bowl of chili.

—ALLEGED DYING WORDS OF KIT CARSON

Nervous? I feel like a pizza on the way to Roseanne Barr!

—ANONYMOUS

Popcorn is the sentimental good-time Charlie of American foods.

—PATRICIA LINDEN

The greatest dog in the world is a hot dog—it feeds the hand that bites it.

—ANONYMOUS

Too few people understand a really good sandwich.

—JAMES BEARD

Pastrami is the meat of love.

—BRIAN HACKETT, "WINGS"

My favorite sandwich is peanut butter, baloney, cheddar cheese, lettuce, and mayonnaise on toasted bread with catsup on the side.

—HUBERT H. HUMPHREY

It has been well said that a hungry man is more interested in four sandwiches than four freedoms.

—HENRY CABOT LODGE, JR.

GLOBAL GOODIES

The trouble with eating Italian food is that five or six days later you're hungry again.

—GEORGE MILLER

The destiny of nations depends on their manner of eating.

—BRILLAT-SAVARIN

Everything you see, I owe to spaghetti.

—SOPHIA LOREN

In France, cooking is a serious art form and a national sport.

—THE NEW YORK TIMES

Romanian-Yiddish cooking has killed more Jews than Hitler.

—ZERO MOSTEL

French cuisine is so delicious that it's a tribute to Gallic willpower that Frenchmen ever leave the dinner table and attend to business.

—HENRY O'DORMAN

If the Japanese are such technological giants, why do they still eat with sticks?

—ANONYMOUS

Following the Romanian tradition, garlic is used in excess to keep the vampires away.

—CALVIN TRILLIN

On the continent people have good food; in England people have good table manners.

—GEORGE MIKES

How come the Germans have lived next door to the French all those years without having acquired any of the magnificent knack for preparing food?

—MISS MANNERS (JUDITH MARTIN)

France has found a unique way of controlling its unwanted critter population. They have done this by giving unwanted animals like snails, pigeons, and frogs fancy names, thus transforming common backyard pests into expensive delicacies. These are then served to gullible tourists, who will eat anything they can't pronounce.

—CHRIS HARRIS

Italy is like a cooked macaroni—yards and yards of soft tenderness, raveled round everything.

—D. H. LAWRENCE

Japan: A culture based on hot wine and raw fish.

—ANONYMOUS

Sauerkraut and bacon drive all care away.

—GERMAN PROVERB

Please understand the reason why Chinese vegetables taste so good. It is simple. The Chinese do not cook them, they just threaten them!

—JEFF SMITH

Here's a little tip: If your plane is ever hijacked by Muslim terrorists, never order the kosher meal.

—JON STEWART

I'm in favor of liberalizing immigration because of the effect it would have on restaurants. I'd let just about everybody in except the English.

—CALVIN TRILLIN

Bouillabaisse is only good because it is cooked by the French, who, if they cared to try, would produce an excellent and nutritious substitute out of cigar stumps and empty matchboxes.

—NORMAN DOUGLAS

Jews always look for Chinese restaurants, but how often have you heard of a Chinese looking for gefilte fish?

—ANONYMOUS

Never eat Chinese food in Oklahoma.

—BRYAN MILLER

If you're going to America, bring your own food.

—FRAN LEBOWITZ

(British) As a rule they will refuse even to sample a foreign dish, they regard such things as garlic and olive oil with disgust, life is unlivable to them unless they have tea and pudding.

—GEORGE ORWELL

The food in Yugoslavia is fine if you like pork tartare.

—ED BEGLEY, JR.

In England there are sixty different religions, but only one sauce.

—VOLTAIRE

When helicopters were snatching people from the grounds of the American embassy compound during the panic of the final Vietcong push into Saigon, I was sitting in front of the television set shouting, "Get the chefs! Get the chefs!"

—CALVIN TRILLIN

The South excelled in two things which the French deem essential to civilization: a code of manners and a native cuisine.

—JOHN PEALE BISHOP

EXOTIC EATS

I don't go for the nouvelle approach—serving a rabbit rump with coffee extract sauce and a slice of kiwi fruit.

—JEFF SMITH

If'n it comes out of de water and it's not a tree stump or a rock, den it's edible.

—CARLO DINAPOLI

There are some things that sound too funny to eat— guacamole. That sounds like something you yell when you're on fire.

—GEORGE CARLIN

If men ate soufflé before meetings, life could be much different.

—JACQUES BAEYENS

When the taste changes with every bite and the last bite is as good as the first, that's Cajun.

—PAUL PRUDHOMME

Hell, yes, we eat dirt! And if you haven't ever tried blackened red dirt, you don't know what's good!

—ROY BLOUNT, JR.

Cheese steaks . . . are the gastronomic icons of this ethnic city.

—BRYAN MILLER ON PHILADELPHIA

I'm beginning to wonder about him. How can you trust a fella that don't like fricassee of barn owl?

—GRANNY, "THE BEVERLY HILLBILLIES"

Why is not a rat as good as a rabbit? Why should men eat shrimps and neglect cockroaches?

—HENRY WARD BEECHER

In Mexico we have a word for sushi: bait.

—JOSÉ SIMON

Texas does not, like any other region, simply have indigenous dishes. It proclaims them. It congratulates you, on your arrival, at having escaped from the slop pails of the other forty-nine states.

—ALISTAIR COOKE

Inhabitants of undeveloped nations and victims of natural disasters are the only people who have ever been happy to see soybeans.

—FRAN LEBOWITZ

A converted cannibal is one who, on Friday, eats only fishermen.

—EMILY LOTNEY

Tofu—what is that stuff? It's like spackling compound. It's like chickpeas and grout. Food should not caulk windows.

—ANONYMOUS

Fondue is out of style. It's like the leisure suit of the food world.

—JULI HESS

DINING OUT

I never eat in a restaurant that's over a hundred feet off the ground and won't stand still.

—CALVIN TRILLIN

Where you eat is sacred.

—MEL BROOKS

Better a good dinner than a fine coat.

—FRENCH PROVERB

Dining is and always was a great artistic opportunity.
—FRANK LLOYD WRIGHT

People are getting tired of going out to expensive restaurants and spending lots of money for seven pea pods and a two-inch steak.
—LYNNE BIEN

He who eats alone chokes alone.
—ARAB PROVERB

Sharing food with another human being is an intimate act that should not be indulged in lightly.
—M. F. K. FISHER

One finds companions for food and drink, but in a serious business a man's companions are very few.
—THEOGNIS

Never trust the food in a restaurant on top of the tallest building in town that spends a lot of time folding napkins.
—ANDY ROONEY

Dinner theater is anti-culture.
—JOHN SIMON

A café is not a filling station for fueling the human engine with a quick shot of caffeine; it is a way station where travelers may dawdle for ten minutes or three hours as their dispositions and appointment calendars demand.

—JOSEPH MAZO

Living is a dangerous business, and simple pleasures should not be denied. I for one plan to enjoy my fettucine Alfredo.

—GABE MEJIAS

A gourmet restaurant in Cincinnati is one where you leave the tray on the table after you eat.

—ANONYMOUS

If the soup had been as warm as the wine, and the wine as old as the fish, and the fish as young as the maid, and the maid as willing as the hostess, it would have been a very good meal.

—ANONYMOUS

Show me another pleasure like dinner, which comes every day and lasts an hour.

—CHARLES DE TALLEYRAND

A restaurant is a fantasy—a kind of living fantasy in which diners are the most important members of the cast.

—WARNER LEROY

Strange to see how a good dinner and feasting reconciles everybody.

—SAMUEL PEPYS

Dinnertime is the most wonderful period of the day and perhaps its goal—the blossoming of the day. Breakfast is the bud.

—NOVALIS

Just ten years ago, the odds of finding sophisticated food in Las Vegas were slightly less than the chances of financing a child's college education on the roulette wheel.

—BRYAN MILLER

Americans are just beginning to regard food the way the French always have. Dinner is not what you do in the evening before something else. Dinner is the evening.

—ART BUCHWALD

I never eat when I can dine.

—MAURICE CHEVALIER

The best number for a dinner party is two—myself and a dam' good headwaiter.

—NUBAR GULBENKIAN

If Jesus Christ were to come today, people would not even crucify him. They would ask him to dinner, and hear what he had to say, and make fun of it.

—THOMAS CARLYLE

A banquet is probably the most fatiguing thing in the world except ditchdigging.

—MARK TWAIN

PASSION FOOD

And I never went to work without a sprig of basil in my cleavage. Men like a woman who smells like good food.
—Eighty-six-year-old Rose Pistola

There is nothing like good food, good wine, and a bad girl.
—Fortune cookie

Truffles . . . quite possibly the world's sexiest food. You never forget your first one, or stop hungering for your next.
—Sally Schneider

Great food is like great sex—the more you have the more you want.
—GAEL GREENE

Too many cooks spoil the brothel.
—MADAME POLLY ADLER

Sex is good, but not as good as fresh sweet corn.
—GARRISON KEILLOR

Without bread, without wine, love is nothing.
—FRENCH PROVERB

The way to a man's heart is through his stomach.
—FANNY FARMER

Truffles make the women more tender and the men more passionate.
—BRILLAT-SAVARIN

Nothing takes the taste out of peanut butter quite like unrequited love.
—CHARLIE BROWN

Eating food with a knife and fork is like making love through an interpreter.

—ANONYMOUS

All real men love to eat.

—MARLENE DIETRICH

The right diet directs sexual energy into the parts that matter.

—BARBARA CARTLAND

Making love without love is like trying to make a soufflé without eggs.

—SIMONE BECK

Love and eggs should be fresh to be enjoyed.

—RUSSIAN PROVERB

Love never dies of starvation but often of indigestion.

—NINON DE LENCLOS

For the millions of us who live glued to computer keyboards at work and TV monitors at home, food may be more than entertainment. It may be the only sensual experience left.

—Barbara Ehrenreich

Cooking is like love. It should be entered into with abandon or not at all.

—Harriet Van Horne

Anyone who eats three meals a day should understand why cookbooks outsell sex books, three to one.

—L. M. Boyd

I prefer girls who are young. When I eat a peach, I don't want it overripe. I want that peach when it's peaking.

—Jim Brown

Love doesn't just sit there, like a stone; it had to be made, like bread, remade all the time, made new.

—Ursula K. Le Guin

u get to fifty-two, food becomes more than sex.

—Prue Leith

Old age is when you look the food over, instead of the waitress.

—ANONYMOUS

No mean woman can cook well, for it calls for a light head, a generous spirit, and a large heart.

—PAUL GAUGUIN

My husband says I feed him like he's a god; every meal is a burnt offering.

—RHONDA HANSON

I'm at the age where food has taken the place of sex in my life. In fact, I've just had a mirror put over my kitchen table.

—RODNEY DANGERFIEl·

Chili's a lot like sex: When it's good it's great, and even when it's bad, it's not bad.

—BILL BOLDENWECK

Hot pepper sauces may be the only products that proudly advertise on their labels how much pain they're going to cause you.

—*MEN'S HEALTH*

Being good in bed means I'm propped up with pillows and my mom brings me soup.

—BROOKE SHIELDS

FOOD FOR THOUGHT

Often I think the main point of life is having something to talk about at dinner.

—JERRY HALL

It isn't so much what's on the table that matters as what's on the chairs.

—WILLIAM GILBERT

Flops are a part of life's menu, and I've never been a girl to miss out on any of the courses.

—ROSALIND RUSSELL

Conversation is the enemy of good wine and food.
—ALFRED HITCHCOCK

When my grandfather was a boy, fast food meant the ones you couldn't catch.
—ANONYMOUS

We must eat to live and live to eat.
—HENRY FIELDING

If brains was lard, Jethro couldn't grease a pan.
—JED CLAMPETT, "THE BEVERLY HILLBILLIES"

If a man be sensible and one fine morning, while he is lying in bed, count at the tips of his fingers how many things in this life truly will give him enjoyment, invariably he will find food is the first one.
—LIN YUTANG

I am not a glutton. I am an explorer of food.
—ERMA BOMBECK

He who steals my money gets trash; he who steals my food gets a good meal.
—ANONYMOUS

The new White House chef is planning on a light menu for Bill Clinton. Yeah, right. This guy will last as long as an Arkansas lawyer.

—DAVID LETTERMAN

Civilization has taught us to eat with a fork, but even now if nobody is around, we use our fingers.

—WILL ROGERS

To eat is human. To digest is divine.

—MARK TWAIN

Food is our common ground, a universal experience.

—JAMES BEARD

Everybody I've talked to seems to agree we should tell our guests if we're serving genetically engineered products.

—KEITH KEOGH, EXECUTIVE CHEF AT EPCOT CENTER
AT DISNEY WORLD

There is no sincerer love than the love of food.

—GEORGE BERNARD SHAW

The halls of the professor and the philosopher are deserted, but what a crowd there is in the cafés.

—LUCIUS ANNAEUS SENECA

It'll be a great day when education gets all the money it wants and the air force has to hold a bake sale to buy bombers.

—ANONYMOUS

Offerings of food have been breaking down barriers for centuries.

—ESTEE LAUDER

As for butter versus margarine, I trust cows more than chemists.

—JOAN GUSSOW

If toast always lands butter side down and cats always land on their feet, what happens if you strap toast on the back of a cat and drop it?

—STEVEN WRIGHT

When the stomach is full it is easy to talk of fasting.

—SAINT JEROME

We urge the administration to use the White House kitchen as a national stage to exemplify a peaceful coexistence of customs and expressions.

—WAYNE NISH AND LYNN FREDERICKS

Man is born to eat.

—CRAIG CLAIBORNE

Feed the people, not the Pentagon.

—BUMPER STICKER

Not only is New York City the nation's melting pot, it is also the casserole, the chafing dish, and the charcoal grill.

—JOHN LINDSAY

Guns will make us powerful; butter will only make us fat.

—HERMANN GOERING

Thought depends absolutely on the stomach, but in spite of that, those who have the best stomachs are not the best thinkers.

—VOLTAIRE

Music with dinner is an insult to both the cook and the violinist.

—G. K. CHESTERTON

Gluttony is an emotional escape, a sign something is eating us.

—PETER DE VRIES

Seeing is deceiving. It's eating that's believing.

—JAMES THURBER

Next to fried food, the South has suffered most from oratory.

—WALTER HINES PAGE

He who does not mind his belly will hardly mind anything else.

—SAMUEL JOHNSON

A good eater must be a good man; for a good eater must have a good digestion, and a good digestion depends upon a good conscience.

—BENJAMIN DISRAELI

Do you think anyone's ever bitten their tongue and then decided to eat the rest?

—DRAKE SATHER

There is more simplicity in the man who eats caviar on impulse than in the man who eats Grape-Nuts on principle.

—G. K. CHESTERTON

Living is like licking honey off a thorn.

—LOUIS ADAMIC

Those who are one in food are one in life.

—MALAGASY PROVERB

A smiling face is half the meal.

—LATIN PROVERB

Food is a weapon.

—MAKSIM LITVINOV

Bad men live that they may eat and drink, whereas good men eat and drink that they may live.

—SOCRATES

A full belly makes a dull brain; the muses starve in a cook's shop.

—BENJAMIN FRANKLIN

In every age its [liberty's] progress has been beset by its natural enemies, by ignorance and superstition, by lust and by love of ease, by the strong man's craving for power, and the poor man's craving for food.

—LORD ACTON

The sinews of war are five—men, money, materials, maintenance [food], and morale.

—BERNARD M. BARUCH

The rule is, jam tomorrow and jam yesterday—but never jam today.

—LEWIS CARROLL

A diet that consists predominantly of rice leads to the use of opium, just as a diet that consists predominantly of potatoes leads to the use of liquor.

—FRIEDRICH NIETZSCHE

Part of the secret of success in life is to eat what you like and let the food fight it out inside.

—MARK TWAIN

An editor is someone who separates the wheat from the chaff and then prints the chaff.

—ADLAI STEVENSON

Chameleons feed on light and air:
Poet's food is love and fame.

—PERCY BYSSHE SHELLEY

If you like to eat potato chips
and chew pork chops on clipper ships
I suggest that you chew a few chips and a chop
at Skipper Zipp's Clipper Ship Chip Chop Shop

—DR. SEUSS

The world is an ugly place. You could get slaughtered by a gang of punks on your way to work. So do what I do. Eat every meal as if it were your last. One of these days, it's gonna be.

—CALVERT DeFOREST

It's part of the Texas ritual. We're rich as son-of-a-bitch stew but look how homely we are, just as plain-folksy as Grandpappy back in 1836. We know about champagne and caviar but we talk hog and hominy.

—EDNA FERBER

We have not journeyed all this way across the centuries, across the oceans, and across the mountains, across the prairies, because we are made of sugar candy.

—WINSTON CHURCHILL

The healthy stomach is nothing if it is not conservative. Few radicals have good digestions.

—SAMUEL BUTLER

The act of putting into your mouth what the earth has grown is perhaps your most direct interaction with the earth.

—FRANCES MOORE LAPPÉ

A man seldom thinks with more earnestness of anything than he does of his dinner.

—SAMUEL JOHNSON

To eat is to appropriate by destruction.

—JEAN-PAUL SARTRE

Man is the only animal that can remain on friendly terms with the victims he intends to eat until he eats them.

—SAMUEL BUTLER

Most of those who make collections of verse or epigrams are like men eating cherries or oysters; they choose out the best at first, and end by eating all.

—SÉBASTIEN-ROCH NICOLAS DE CHAMFORT

The shelf life of the modern hardback writer is some-where between the milk and the yogurt.

—JOHN MORTIMER

Genuine polemics approach a book as lovingly as a canni-bal spices a baby.

—WALTER BENJAMIN

As long as mixed grills and combination salads are popu-lar, anthologies will undoubtedly continue in favor.

—ELIZABETH JANEWAY

It is as healthy to enjoy sentiment as to enjoy jam.

—G. K. CHESTERTON

I've run more risk eating my way across the country than in all my driving.

—DUNCAN HINES

Comedy just pokes at problems, rarely confronts them squarely. Drama is like a plate of meat and potatoes, comedy is rather the dessert, a bit like meringue.

—WOODY ALLEN

I pity them greatly, but I must be mum,
For how could we do without sugar and rum?
—WILLIAM COWPER

Everything is a miracle. It is a miracle that one does not dissolve in one's bath like a lump of sugar.
—PABLO PICASSO

Warm cookies and cold milk are good for you.
—ROBERT FULGHUM

If you have to eat crow, eat it while it's hot.
—ALBEN BARKLEY

Better to sleep with a sober cannibal than a drunken Christian.
—HERMAN MELVILLE

The best use of fat since the invention of bacon.
—RAY SONS ON CHICAGO BEARS FOOTBALL PLAYER
WILLIAM "REFRIGERATOR" PERRY

I tried to emulate them, but I think I was sort of like a dessert, you know, crêpes suzette or something like that. But they were potatoes and meat. Strong, simple, and not fancy.
—KATHARINE HEPBURN ON HER LEADING MEN

The world is an oyster, but you don't crack it open on a mattress.
—ARTHUR MILLER

Criticizing someone's favorite neighborhood Chinese restaurant is like criticizing their children. They can. You can't.
—ARTHUR SCHWARTZ

Who goes to bed supperless tosses all night.
—ITALIAN PROVERB

When the guests at a gathering are well acquainted, they eat twenty percent more than they otherwise would.
—EDGAR W. HOWE

Men that can have communication in nothing else can sympathetically eat together, can still rise into some glow of brotherhood over food and wine.

—THOMAS CARLYLE

Whenever I get married, I start buying *Gourmet* magazine.

—NORA EPHRON

I am not interested in picking up crumbs of compassion thrown from the table of someone who considers himself my master. I want the full menu of rights.

—BISHOP DESMOND TUTU

Society is composed of two great classes—those who have more dinners than appetite, and those who have more appetite than dinners.

—SÉBASTIEN-ROCH NICOLAS DE CHAMFORT

For an artist to marry his model is as fatal as for a gourmet to marry his cook: The one gets no sittings. And the other gets no dinners.

—OSCAR WILDE

Your food is close to your stomach, but you must put it in your mouth first.

—WEST AFRICAN SAYING

You catch more flies with honey than you do with vinegar.

—ANONYMOUS

Never argue at the dinner table, for the one who is not hungry always gets the best of the argument.

—RICHARD WHATELY

It doesn't matter who rules. I just want to get my vegetables to market.

—CHINESE PEASANT IN GANSU PROVINCE

What hunger is in relation to food, zest is in relation to life.

—BERTRAND RUSSELL

Fame is a fickle food upon a shifting plate.

—EMILY DICKINSON

A true gastronome should always be ready to eat, just as a soldier should always be ready to fight.

—CHARLES MONSELET

Hunger is the handmaid of genius.

—MARK TWAIN

No man is lonely while eating spaghetti; it requires so much attention.

—Christopher Morley

Culture is what your butcher would have if he were a surgeon.

—Mary Poole

You needn't tell me that a man who doesn't love oysters and asparagus and good wines has got a soul.

—Saki

I won't eat anything that has intelligent life, but I'd gladly eat a network executive or a politician.

—Marty Feldman

Those who feed on politics learn to dine on baloney.
—JAMES J. KILPATRICK

Lips however rosy must be fed.
—FRENCH PROVERB

At a dinner party one should eat wisely but not too well, and talk well but not too wisely.
—W. SOMERSET MAUGHAM

When I write of hunger, I am really writing about love and the hunger for it, and warmth and the love of it . . . and it is all one.
—M. F. K. FISHER

My mouth is a happy place.
—PAT CONROY

An army marches on its stomach.
—NAPOLEON BONAPARTE

Tell me what you eat and I will tell you what you are.
—BRILLAT-SAVARIN

The first thing I remember liking that liked me back was food.

—Rhoda Morgenstern

Never invest your money in anything that eats or that needs repairing.

—Billy Rose

Business without profit is not business any more than a pickle is candy.

—Charles F. Abbott

An expert is like the bottom of a double boiler. It shoots off a lot of steam, but it never really knows what's cooking.

—anonymous

A man without a hearty appetite at the table won't have a good appetite for anything else.

—anonymous

In Hollywood the favorite word is "sex"; in the Midwest it is "cheese"; in the South, "honey"; in Manhattan, "money."

—Amy Vanderbilt

Health and appetite impart the sweetness to sugar, bread, and meat.

—RALPH WALDO EMERSON

The man who has scalded his lips on milk will blow on his ice cream.

—TURKISH PROVERB

Physicians, like beer, are best when they are old, and lawyers, like bread, when they are young and new.

—ANONYMOUS

God makes the milk but not the pail.

—GERMAN PROVERB

When it rains honey and milk the poor man has no spoon.

—MONTENEGRIN PROVERB

Words do not make flour.

—ITALIAN PROVERB

Never eat at a place called Mom's. Never play cards with a man named Doc. And never lie down with a woman who's got more troubles than you.

—NELSON ALGREN

A wise man does not trust all his eggs to one basket.
—CERVANTES

Let us eat and drink; for tomorrow we shall die.
—THE BIBLE, ISAIAH 22:13

A feast is made for laughter, and wine maketh merry.
—THE BIBLE, ECCLESIASTES

More die in the United States of too much food than of too little.
—JOHN KENNETH GALBRAITH

Oats—a grain, which in England is generally given to horses, but in Scotland supports the people.
—SAMUEL JOHNSON

[I] would rather live in Russia on black bread and vodka than in the United States at the best hotels. America knows nothing of food, love, or art.
—ISADORA DUNCAN

This recipe is certainly silly. It says to separate eggs, but it doesn't say how far to separate them.
—GRACIE ALLEN

The quality of food is in inverse proportion to the altitude of the dining room, with airplanes the extreme example.
— BRYAN MILLER

Small cheer and great welcome makes a merry feast.
— WILLIAM SHAKESPEARE

Eggs of an hour, bread of a day, wine of a year, a friend of thirty years.
— ITALIAN PROVERB

Food is the most primitive form of comfort.
— SHEILAH GRAHAM

Food is to eat, not to frame and hang on the wall.
— WILLIAM DENTON

Give me books, fruit, French wine, and fine weather, and a little music out of doors, played by someone I do not know.
— JOHN KEATS

Once we sowed wild oats, now we cook them in the microwave.
— ANONYMOUS

Man does not live by words alone, despite the fact that sometimes he has to eat them.

—ADLAI STEVENSON

Borscht and bread make your cheeks red.

—JEWISH PROVERB

Soup and fish explain half the emotions of human life.

—SYDNEY SMITH

Almost every person has something secret he likes to eat.

—M. F. K. FISHER

Summer cooking implies a sense of immediacy, a capacity to capture the essence of the fleeting moment.

—ELIZABETH DAVID

An epicure is one who gets nothing better than the cream of everything, but cheerfully makes the best of it.

—OLIVER HEREFORD

We are rarely ill, and if we are, we go off somewhere and eat grass until we feel better.

—PAUL GALLICO

I am not a gourmet chick.

—PEARL BAILEY

Eating is touch carried to the bitter end.

—SAMUEL BUTLER

Eat butter first, and eat it last, and live till a hundred years be past.

—OLD DUTCH PROVERB

You either eat or you are eaten.

—DIDIER RABATTU

All I ask of food is that it doesn't harm me.

—MICHAEL PALIN

Let food be your medicine and medicine be your food.
—HIPPOCRATES

Wisdom is like an open oven: The food is gone, but the heat remains.

—ANONYMOUS

To a man with an empty stomach, food is God.
—MOHANDAS (MAHATMA) GANDHI

Hunger makes a thief of any man.

—PEARL S. BUCK

You cannot feed the hungry on statistics.
—DAVID LLOYD GEORGE

Hunger is not debatable.

—HARRY HOPKINS

Hunger is the best sauce in the world.

—CERVANTES

If you ask a hungry man how much is two and two, he replies "four loaves."

—HINDU PROVERB

When the stomach is empty, so is the brain.

—YIDDISH PROVERB

You cannot reason with a hungry belly; it has no ears.

—GREEK PROVERB

Grub first, then mortality.

—BERTHOLT BRECHT

Undoubtedly, the desire for food has been, and still is, one of the main causes of great political events.
—BERTRAND RUSSELL

Starvation, not sin, is the parent of modern crime.
—OSCAR WILDE

Hungry men have no respect for law, authority, or human life.
—MARCUS GARVEY

A hungry man is not a free man.
—ADLAI STEVENSON

A hungry people listens not to reason, nor cares for justice, nor is bent by any prayers.
—SENECA THE YOUNGER

Let food be your medicine and medicine be your food.
—HIPPOCRATES

Food is our common ground; a universal experience.
—JAMES BEARD

Ron Fuchs has dined around the world,
but home cooking, followed by a bowl (or two)
of ice cream, still tops his culinary list.
This is his first book.